TO BE A CATHOLIC
A CATECHISM FOR TODAY

TO BE A CATHOLIC

A Catechism for Today

by

Joseph V. Gallagher, C.S.P.

PAULIST PRESS
New York/Paramus/Toronto

NIHIL OBSTAT:
Rev. Anthony T. Padovano
Censor Librorum

IMPRIMATUR:
✚ Thomas A. Boland, S.T.D.
Archbishop of Newark

August 24, 1970

The Nihil Obstat and Imprimatur are official declarations that a book or pamphlet is free of doctrinal or moral error. No implication is contained therein that those who have granted the Nihil Obstat and Imprimatur agree with the contents, opinions or statements expressed.

Library of Congress
Catalog Card Number: 73-137884

Published by Paulist Press
Editorial Office: 1865 Broadway, New York, N.Y. 10023.
Business Office: Paramus, New Jersey 07652

Printed and bound in the
United States of America

CONTENTS

CONTENTS

INTRODUCTION

Religion and God

Religion means different things to different people. Men vary not only in what they believe but also in the importance they attach to it and the way in which religion fits into their lives. This catechism is concerned with the Catholic religion, but, for a beginning, it is worth looking at religion generally because its principal characteristics are also found in Catholicism.

Like religion, God too means different things to people. Sometimes it is only a word and means little to the person using it. Some people can talk seriously about God without believing in him. Others can believe in him and never talk about him. In some religions, God occupies a more important place than in others, and there are religions that hardly need him at all. The Catholic religion thinks God is the most important of all realities, but it also realizes that men do not always see this, and that even when they do, it is never easy to be clear about God.

1. What does religion do to man?

Religion takes man out of the limitations of his own world and relates him to something bigger and more mysterious.

1

2. Is religion always beneficial?

No. Sometimes instead of freeing man from his limitations, it can impose new restrictions on his well-being and development. Degrading superstitions and taboos have often been imposed in the name of religion.

3. What attracts people to religion?

Humanly speaking, people respond to what promises to liberate them and to enlarge their capacity to live. Men need to be reassured about some basic things if they are to live with joy and freedom.

4. What do people need to be reassured about?

Deep down, people have to know who they are. They also need to feel a sense of belonging and a sense of purpose, and to know that their lives are important no matter what happens. Finally, we all want the reassurance that death does not simply undo everything we have done in life. All religion tries in some way to reassure people about these things.

5. Is this true of the Christian religion and of Catholics?

Yes. Christians and Catholics are human beings, too.

6. Is religion a human thing?

In the sense that it meets a basic human need, yes. But if religion succeeds in tying man into something outside himself, then it goes beyond the human and involves questions about God.

7. What is God?

God is the name men usually give to the origin and meaning of existence.

8. Is God real?

Yes. A great many people have discovered that the final explanation of existence is an all-powerful being existing above and beyond man and his world. They frequently differ on what this being is like.

9. When is God unreal?

When he is the product of man's invention. Some ideas about God are distorted and confused. They are usually exaggerations of something people have heard about God. Human imagination and feelings put together a picture of something called "God" that is far removed from the reality.

10. What are some unreal gods?

There have been thousands in man's history.

Some modern examples that confuse Christians
are: (a) a "magical God" who makes everything
all right when the right words are said and the
right buttons pushed; (b) a "law and order God"
who runs the world by a very strict code of
behavior and whose main concern is to judge;
(c) a "cat and mouse God" who has everybody's
whole life laid out in front of him and who makes
things happen to people for reasons of his own.
There are many other false gods, but none of
them is the Christian God.

11. When is God real?

The true God is always real. He becomes real for
us when we come to know him for the person he
is. We can only do this from what he has shown
us of himself.

12. Why is God's self-revelation important?

We get to know people as they really are only
through what they show of themselves. To know
God personally, we have to be carefully attentive
to whatever he shows of himself.

13. How does God show himself?

In all of life, creation, and history. However, the
Christian religion and the Catholic Church are
especially concerned with a very personal way
in which God showed and continues to show

himself to men. This revelation is described in the Bible, and from it the Catholic derives both his explanation of life and a way of living.

I

THE REAL CHRISTIAN GOD

The Christian is convinced that God is real. He believes that the final explanation of who man is and what his life means is to be found in another person —one who is only partly known, mysterious and powerful. How a Christian reaches this conviction is the central plot of his personal life story. Usually it results from a mixture of religious upbringing, life experience, and the inner sense of a presence other than himself. Based upon this faith, a Catholic would answer the most important questions about life in the following way:

1. Who am I?

I am someone who belongs to greatness. God is my Father.

2. Does my life really mean something?

Yes. God my Father has given it to me. I belong to him; he loves me and asks me to love him. Thus, I have something to live for that deserves the best I have.

3. What part do I play in the world where I live?

God my Father made this world and the whole

universe. He put me in it and I take much of my life from it. As I grow to love my Father, I find that I put much of myself into his world and help it to grow, too.

4. Can the life of man and the world really come to something?

Yes. God our Father who made all is extremely powerful.

5. How do I know I belong to God?

God's Son, Jesus Christ, came into human life as my brother to teach me this and to show me what it means to belong to God.

6 What did Jesus reveal about the Son of God?

Jesus showed in his life and teaching that the Son is powerful and good like his Father.

7. What did Jesus show about belonging to God?

Jesus' whole life was devoted to doing the work and will of his Father. This teaches me that to belong to God means to be like Jesus.

8. Why is it important to have God as a Father?

Because God my Father gives me life and love

and, in so doing, makes me forever part of
something bigger than myself.

9. **How can I live up to this inheritance?**

My Father gives me God the Holy Spirit to live
within me and to guide me in communicating
with the Father, to help me understand his words,
and to make my life and my love like that of
Jesus (John 16:12-15).

10. **Who is God?**

God is my Father, my Brother Jesus Christ, and
the Holy Spirit. These incomparably perfect
persons share an unending life of mutual love
and creative power. Together they are the one I
call God (John 14:8-17).

11. **Why does God have three different names?**

God's life is so filled with vitality and love that
three persons must live it. The names of these
persons have been given us by Jesus.

12. **What do these names mean?**

We associate the names of each person with
different experiences we have of God. God,
giving us all that we have, we call "Father."
God, showing himself to man, we call "Son."
God, living within us, we call "Holy Spirit."

13. To whom do I belong?

My life belongs with the persons closest to me: God, my Father; Jesus Christ, my Lord and Savior; the Holy Spirit, my inner teacher and guide. I also share my life with my family, friends, co-workers and all the people who cross my path.

14. How do I know death won't undo all of this?

Jesus Christ has saved me from that fate. Because of him the Father shares his unending life with me, and the Holy Spirit will make me so like Jesus that, even though I die, my Father will again raise me to life as he did his Son, Jesus Christ.

15. What is the purpose of my life?

To respond to my Father's loving invitation by coming to know him and growing in love of him and giving myself to him in the service of others.

16. When will my purpose be achieved?

It is achieved every time I say "yes" to his invitation. Its final achievement comes when I give myself completely over to him at my death.

In such a way a Catholic puts into words what his faith teaches him about the farthest horizons of his

9

life. Like most men he sometimes experiences a mysterious presence deep within him. From this experience he senses that the boundaries of his life are not as clear-cut as they seem on the surface. He senses, too, that much of importance to him lies just out of reach, deep in that mysterious presence. However, this experience does not provide the words he puts down in answer. In fact, it gives no words or names at all. The names "Father," "Son," and "Holy Spirit" come from his Church who first heard them from Jesus. The Catholic connects them to these questions because somewhere along the line he has come to recognize that the loving God named by Jesus and that mysterious inner presence are one and the same.

II

JESUS CHRIST: MAN AND GOD

*Men come to believe in God because he shows
something of himself to them. Somehow through the
tangle of people, events, experience, and challenge
that is life they catch a glimpse of someone who is in
it, yet beyond it, and begin to reach out in response
to him. All real faith is the result of some such
personal meeting between God and man.*

*Christians believe because they are sure that God
shows himself in a fully personal way in Jesus Christ.
In Jesus he shows himself the same way a human
person does, i.e., in what he says and does, how he
reacts to others, by what he conveys of his thoughts
and feelings. In the person of Jesus Christ, God
reveals as much of himself as man can grasp.*

*For this reason Jesus is the center of Christian faith.
In him the Christian finds God and comes to believe
In him. Because of this, everything about Jesus is
important. What he said and did, the way he lived and
died, what his friends discovered about him—all
these are important to the Christian faith because
they reveal to us the presence and power of God
our Father.*

Jesus Christ is our way, our truth, and our life.

1. Why is Jesus important?

Because he is the door to God. In discovering him, we meet God in a human being and actually see his love for us in practice. We understand what Jesus teaches and the things he does because they are well-known human words and actions. But there is more. Finding him, we step also into the mysterious presence of our Father (John 10:7-10).

2. Who is Jesus Christ?

He is God, the Son of the Father, who became a man (John 8:42-59).

3. Is Jesus human?

Yes. The Son became a real man. This means he was born into this world, and lived a real human life, and died like the rest of us (Luke 2:1-7).

4. When and where did he live?

About two thousand years ago in Israel, then a part of the Roman Empire.

5. Who were his parents?

His mother was a young girl named Mary. He had no human father. Instead, he was directly conceived by the Holy Spirit within Mary and thereafter was born in the normal course of events. Because of this extraordinary action of God, Mary has been called ever since the "Blessed Virgin" (Luke 1:26-38).

6. Who was Joseph?

Joseph was Mary's husband and acted as foster father to Jesus during his childhood.

7. What do we know about Jesus' life?

We know very little about his early years. However, when he reached manhood we know he spent several years traveling about Israel, teaching the people about his Father's love for them and performing extraordinary cures and other wonders. We know, too, that his activities brought him into conflict with the religious leaders of the Jewish people and that they finally arranged for his execution by the Roman authorities.

8. Where do we find this data?

Principally, in the four gospel books of the New Testament.

9. Was Jesus' death the end of him?

No. His Father raised him up to life within a few days and he showed himself to many of his

followers for some time after that, reassuring
them that he really lived and reemphasizing what
he had taught them before. Then he ended his
appearances and lives now in the glory of God
(Mark 16).

10. What is the main point of Jesus' teaching?

Jesus' message was that with him the kingdom
of God had come into the world. This means that
God's own way of life has been initiated among
men and they are called to enter it, living and
working in partnership with God for the growth
and completion of the kingdom (Mark 1:14-15).

11. What did Jesus teach about God's way of life?

He taught that God's life is love. God lives by
forever giving himself. To belong to the kingdom
means that a man must live by love, too. Like
Jesus, we must be willing to live for others
(1 John 4:7-16).

12. How does Jesus teach God's love?

Jesus teaches people by describing his Father.
More importantly, his very life is a lesson in
which men can see God's love at work. Jesus
Christ in his person, life and teaching shows us
God-giving-himself to man (John 16:25-28).

13. What does Jesus ask of those who listen to him?

He asks that men turn out from themselves and

their past and accept him as the keystone of their lives for the future. This turning to Jesus is called "conversion" (John 3:31-36).

14. What does it take for such a "conversion"?

Conversion requires the conviction that God is the full measure and meaning of life and that Jesus Christ is the door to God (Acts 2:36-39).

15. What is the point of departure for Christian faith?

That Jesus Christ is God-become-man who died in serving us and brought us to new life through his resurrection (I Cor. 15:12-19).

16. Why do Christians believe?

Because in Jesus Christ they have come to see the goodness and love of God perfectly at work in the life of man (I John 1:1-7).

III

THE HISTORY OF GOD'S LOVE FOR MAN

The life, death, and resurrection of Jesus is the decisive event of all time through which God shows himself and his love for man. However, he also shows himself in lesser ways in other events.

Probably, if men were sensitive enough to God they would be able to see something of him in everything. As it is, over the centuries certain special events have been recognized as signs of God by men of faith. They see something of God in these events because they are already close to him and sensitive to his presence. When he is recognized in an event, his people speak out and their word declares to all what God is communicating through the happening. In this fashion, certain special events, past and present, are a part of the Christian faith.

These events are found in the Bible and in the life of the Church. They are decisive for the Christian in his relationship with God. He cannot explain or live his faith apart from them.

The Bible and the Church are witnesses to these events. They testify to their occurrence and explain their meaning. Hence, Bible and Church are both essential for the Christian.

(a) THE BIBLE

1. What is the Bible?

The Bible is a collection of books written under
the inspiration of God about a particular people's
experience of God.

2. Who wrote the Bible?

The Bible was written by many people, all men
of faith, most of whose names are lost to us, over
a long period of time and, in most cases, well
after the experiences recounted.

3. What is the Old Testament?

The forty-six books of the Old Testament contain
a history of the Jewish people and their faith
from earliest origins down to the first century.
They also include books of poems and prayers,
laws and stories, books of wisdom and practical
advice in the art of living.

4. Where did the material come from?

It all came from the life and experience of the
Jewish people. Much of the material was passed
along by word of mouth for generations before it
was finally collected, worked together, and
written the way we now have it.

5. What is the New Testament?

The New Testament is the record of what the early followers of Jesus had to say about him and his teaching.

6. What does the New Testament include?

The New Testament includes four gospels or basic preachings of Jesus' followers. Each of these differs in approach and detail according to the personality and purposes of the authors, but they all tell of Jesus and his teaching. The New Testament also contains a history of the early Church (Acts), twenty-one letters of the apostles (epistles), and a book of prophecy (Apocalypse).

7. Where did the material come from?

It all came from the earliest communities of Jesus' followers.

8. Is the Bible historically accurate?

Not always. Records were scarce in those centuries and people were little concerned or equipped for approaching history scientifically. The accounts are accurate enough for the overall history they contain.

9. Is the Bible true?

Yes. Essentially the Bible is the testimony of

what God has done in the life of a people and
what they have come to believe about him
through this experience. That testimony is clear,
consistent, and true. This faith **really** happened.

10. Is any of the Bible outdated?

Yes. Much of the language and ideas it contains
belongs to another age and culture and is no
longer in use. The Bible's understanding of
nature and the universe is very primitive and
hopelessly behind modern science. Even many of
its religious laws and practices mean little to
modern man. These things make it difficult for us
to read it easily today and we need expert help
to understand it.

11. Why is the Bible important?

It is the written record of God's decisive actions
in the world. These disclose the meaning of life
and point the way to man's future. Nothing is
more important to man than this kind of vision
and hope.

12. What does it have to say about life here and now?

While the Bible expresses principally a **past**
experience of God, it has a present vitality, too.
When read prayerfully it can communicate a
here and now presence and action of God to the

attentive listener. Moreover, the experience of these men of faith lights up whole areas of our own lives and helps us discover new directions and meaning around us. In this way, God continually challenges and invites men to enter the world of faith.

(b) GOD IN THE LIFE OF MAN

13. What are the key acts of God in the life of man?

First, he gave life and the world to man; next, he helped men to discover a true direction and purpose; then, he personally entered the life of man and invited man to life with him; finally, he communicates his own life to those who accept his invitation.

14. How did he give life and the world to man?

The Bible calls it "creation." We don't know **how** it happened. Science explores that process and may yet explain it fully to us. At present, it seems to have been a gradual evolutionary development that took place a very long time ago. But however he gave it to us, the important thing for faith is that we owe all that we have to God (Gen. 1:1-2).

15. Does the Bible try to explain creation?

Not really. God's people knew that he was Lord of life and the universe. This they could assert, but millions of years after the event they could only imagine how creation took place.

16. How did God help man to discover a true direction and purpose?

The decisive education of man as to who he really is and what he can become is detailed in the Old Testament. There, we see a long and painful educational process as God introduces himself to man and urges man to open himself to God and to his own future.

17. How did God enter man's life and invite man to share his?

He personally became a man in Jesus Christ who then summoned his fellow men to the kingdom of his Father.

18. How does God communicate his life to others?

Through the Holy Spirit whom he sends to live within his friends (John 14:15-17).

(c) GOD'S ACTION IN THE OLD TESTAMENT

19. How did God begin his action in the Old Testament?

He began about 4,000 years ago with a man

named Abraham. Abraham responded to his
summons and followed him all of his life.
Because of Abraham's faithfulness, God chose
his descendants to be his own special people
(Gen. 12:1-7).

20. Who were God's people?

The Jewish people, known in the Old Testament
as "Israel."

21. Where did they come from?

They came out of Egypt. Originally their
ancestors had come there as refugees from
famine and stayed on. However, after several
generations the Egyptians turned on them and
enslaved them.

22. How did they get out of Egypt?

God inspired Moses to convince these people
that if they put their trust in the God of their
fathers he would lead them out of slavery and
into a land of their own. The long and difficult
emigration that followed is called the "Exodus"
(Ex. 12:21-42).

23. How did they become God's people?

After their escape they wandered through the

Sinai desert. Moses reminded them that their successful liberation was due to their trust in God who inspired it. God had called them out of Egypt to become his own people and it was time to express their trust in permanent form. After much prayer and exhortation by Moses and much hesitation and resistance from the people, they solemnly declared their acceptance of God and their willingness to be his people (Ex. 19:1-8).

24. How did they express this?

They held a solemn ceremony and sealed their commitment to God in the blood of animals. These animals had been killed and offered to God as gifts (Ex. 24:3-8).

25. What is this commitment called?

The "Covenant." A covenant was an ancient legal form by which a king's sovereignty over a people was recognized and accepted by them. Israel differed from the other nations because **her** covenant was with God.

26. What were the conditions of the Covenant?

They were expressed in the ten commandments which Moses presented to the people. This was to be their basic law. It spelled out their obligations to God and to each other. As time went on, other laws were added so that the whole life of the people was organized around their promise to God (Ex. 20:1-17).

27. Did Israel keep the Covenant?

No, they constantly broke it by abandoning God and ignoring his commandments. This contradiction of their commitment led them into war, suffering and defeat. They learned faithfulness only through long and hard experience.

28. Did God keep the Covenant?

Yes. He never abandoned his people and always forgave them when they turned back to him.

29. What did Israel expect of God?

They expected to receive special benefits as his people. They expected in some way to be the instrument through which God would establish his kingdom over the whole world. They also expected they would be first among the nations. Sometimes their expectations were inflated and greedy.

30. What did God finally give his people?

He gave himself. He came among them in the

person of Jesus and announced that the kingdom of God had arrived to stay (John 8:42-47).

31. What did men learn during the period of the Old Testament?

They learned that God was real and the guiding force in their lives. They found that he was faithful to his promises and that men could live as his friends if they put their trust in him.

(d) GOD'S DECISIVE ACT

32. What changes did Jesus bring?

Jesus brought a whole new life to man (John 10:10).

33. What is this new life?

It is God's own life communicated to men by the Holy Spirit who comes to live within them. It is sometimes called "grace" (John 14:18-24).

34. Why is it new?

Because before Jesus came no one loved God enough to be able to live his kind of life.

35. How was Jesus able to do differently?

Because he was the Son of God. Becoming man,

he loved his Father and his fellow men with God's own love.

36. How does his life show this love?

All that he said and did, his whole life and death, was for the sake of others. He spent his life teaching men the truth about his Father and about themselves; he shared their life and suffering and healed their ailments. He did all this out of love for them and for his Father who called him to this service. He stayed with it even when it cost his life.

37. What does Jesus' life teach us about God?

His life shows us in a human way that God's life is a life of love. Father, Son, and Holy Spirit are forever giving themselves to each other.

38. How did the Father respond to Jesus' life?

Having received from Jesus a perfect human life of love, the Father now gives his own life to Jesus' less perfect fellow men who turn to him in faith (Acts 2:22-33).

39. How does a person receive this new life?

By putting his faith, hope and love in Jesus Christ whose life, death and resurrection has

opened up the life of God to man. The Father,
Son, and Holy Spirit come and share their love
with those who commit themselves to Jesus
(Acts 2:37-39).

40. How must a person live the life of God?

As Jesus did. United to him, the Christian must
die to self and rise to a new life for others
(Matt. 16:24-27).

41. Where do we see this gift of new life?

In Jesus' resurrection. He had been brutally
beaten, executed, and buried, but the Father
raised him up to new life and together they give
this new life to Jesus' faithful followers.

42. Will the Father raise us up too?

Yes. Because of Jesus, he loves all of us and
will raise up all who turn to him in faith (I Thess.
4:13-18).

43. When will he do this?

No one knows. When he does it will mean that
God's kingdom among men has been completed
and those who share his life can now share his
glory. This is usually described as the "end of

the world," but it is better thought of as "the fulfillment of God's creation" (Matt. 24:35-44).

44. What is the assumption of Mary?

It is a special grace by which Mary was taken to heaven body and soul where she already enjoys the glory that awaits all of God's faithful children.

45. What is heaven?

Heaven is the name the Church gives to man's life in God after death. In heaven man sees the Father, Son, and Holy Spirit as they truly are and shares their way of life forever. This way of life is mysterious, and we know little about it beyond the fact that it is a state of supreme happiness and joy.

IV

RELATING TO GOD

(1) The Church

The Bible silhouettes for us a world of faith that struggles to surface in the lives of men. To belong to that world is to share in the experience men have of God. To enter the stream of that experience requires some contact with those who live the experience. These persons we call the "Church."

The Church speaks the good news of God's doings in the world. She does this in many ways—through her teaching and preaching, through her life and worship, through her Bible and the writings of her prophets, and through the sometimes halting words of a single Christian expressing his most fundamental hopes. One way or another, it is the Church, past or present, collectively or individually, that puts a name to the question life poses to man and at the same time offers a direction to him in which to pursue his quest.

(a) WHAT THE CHURCH IS

1. How did the Church begin?

The Church began when the Holy Spirit entered

29

into the followers of Jesus and initiated them to the life of God (Acts 2:1-4).

2. When did this happen?

On the day of Pentecost, a Jewish holy day. After his resurrection Jesus showed himself to his closest friends and others of his followers. When they came to believe that he had really conquered death, Jesus withdrew his visible presence and lives on hidden in his Father. On Pentecost he sent his Spirit and life upon his followers as he had promised (Acts 1:1-9).

3. How did Jesus' followers react to the Spirit?

They announced to everybody the good news of what Jesus had done and invited their hearers to believe in him and live by his Spirit (Acts 2:22-24).

4. What is the Church?

The Church is the worldwide community of those whom God has called to give witness to his Son Jesus and to the new life he has brought to man. This assembly has several names, the most common being "the people of God" and "the body of Christ" (Acts 1:6-8).

5. Whom has God called to be witnesses?

Everyone who believes that God has revealed and given himself to men in Jesus Christ.

6. How does the Church give this witness?

By proclaiming in word and deed what God has
done in Jesus. As the community of believers the
Church must live the life of Jesus in his Spirit,
and show his love by her life of brotherhood and
service to others (Acts 3:42-47).

7. What activities make up the Church's witness?

Preaching the Word of God and teaching its
meaning; celebrating God's decisive action in
her liturgy; ministering to the spiritual and
physical needs of men.

**8. How does the Church celebrate God's gift to
man?**

Principally in the Mass and sacraments. In these
ritual acts the Church celebrates what God has
done and thanks him for it.

**9. How does the Church minister to man's
spiritual needs?**

By providing a community of faith, where people
can find support and guidance in their
response to God. Within this community the
Holy Spirit communicates and strengthens the

life of God through the sacraments, prayers, and works of service.

10. What are sacraments?

Special actions in the Church through which the life of God is communicated to his people. In the Catholic Church the sacraments are baptism, confirmation, eucharist, penance, anointing of the sick, holy orders, and matrimony.

11. How does the Church minister to the physical needs of men?

By giving material aid to those in distress and by cooperating with other concerned people in eradicating the causes of suffering and building up a better life for man.

(b) THE UNITY OF THE CHURCH

12. How many churches are there?

There is but one Church. Jesus brought the same news to all men and summoned all to the same new life. His Church is the union of those who follow his call (Eph. 4:1-5).

13. What is the reason for the many churches that exist?

(a) Jesus has many million followers. It is

necessary for them to group together in
different places in communities or
"churches" of manageable size. So there
are many local groupings of the one Church.

(b) Also, in the long history of Christianity
there have been grave differences among
Jesus' followers over the meaning of his
Gospel and the way of living his life. These
have resulted in divisions and the
appearance of separate groups using the
title "Church" with conflicting claims of
fidelity to Jesus and his teaching.

14. Who are these groups?

They are principally the Roman Catholic Church,
the Eastern Orthodox Church, the Anglican
Church, and the various Protestant Churches.
In modern times other groups have originated
independently of these and relate themselves in
different ways to Jesus.

15. What is the Roman Catholic Church?

It is the worldwide community of Jesus'
followers that is united around the Pope.

16. What is the Eastern Orthodox Church?

It is a family of self-governing Christian
communities originating in Eastern Europe and

Asia in the earliest days of Christianity. For a thousand years East and West were united in their following of Jesus, but political, cultural, and theological differences led to a breach in the year 1054. The resulting separation between the Church of the East and of the West has lasted to our own day.

17. What is the Anglican Church?

It is a family of Christian communities that grew out of the 16th-century Reformation in England. The Church in that country asserted her independence of Rome, and the two groups have been separated from one another since. The Episcopal Church is the American member of the Anglican family.

18. What are the Protestant Churches?

They are the continuation or the descendants of those Christian groups which "protested" against certain teachings and practices of the Western Church in the Reformation of the 16th century. Rome and the papacy resisted their protest, and the separation of various groups within the Church followed. Since then further separations have occurred with new groups coming into existence out of these Reformation churches.

19. In what way is the Church one?

There is only one Jesus and he communicates the same life of God to all who believe in him. At this basic level all Christians are truly united and the Church is one.

20. In what way is the Church not one?

Historical differences, enmity, and bitterness have driven the followers of Jesus apart so that much of their Christian life is not shared with one another. Moreover, men's understanding of Jesus and the meaning of his life and teaching differs, and sometimes these differences prevent Christians from coming together. As a result, while the Church is one, this unity cannot be seen in her life and it is not always accepted or understood.

21. What is ecumenism?

It is the acceptance of the basic unity of the Church and the consequent effort to make this unity present and visible in the whole life of the Church.

22. How do other religions fit in?

In Jesus, God came to man in the fullest

possible way. However, he also speaks to men in other ways, and over the centuries men have responded to him under different circumstances. The great religions of the world express some of these different experiences men have had of God.

(c) OFFICES IN THE CHURCH

23. What is the sacrament of holy orders?

It is the act by which the Church chooses and empowers certain individuals to carry out special functions for the building up of Jesus' Church by the power of the Holy Spirit. The major orders of the Church are deacon, priest and bishop.

24. What are the functions of those in holy orders?

The functions vary according to the office an ordained person holds. Generally, they have to do with teaching, administering the sacraments, and governing the Church.

25. What kind of authority does the Church have?

There are two kinds of authority in the Church: the ordinary authority every society has to organize and direct its own affairs, and the special authority given by Jesus to his disciples to teach and act in his name.

26. How does the Church exercise her ordinary authority?

In the usual way of enacting laws to regulate her internal affairs, to promote the good of all, and to fulfill the purposes of the Church.

27. How does she exercise the special authority given by Jesus?

Her teaching, worship, and healing are done in the name of Jesus, and his person and power are present to her when she acts under this authority.

28. Who in the Church exercises authority?

The Pope and the bishops exercise authority for the Church. Others, clergy and laity, can participate in the exercise of the Church's authority in different degrees.

29. Who is the Pope?

He is a visible sign of Jesus and the symbol of unity for the Church. Together with the bishops, and as their head, he is the universal teacher and governor of the Church.

30. Who are the bishops?

They are visible signs of Jesus in each locality and the symbol of unity for the Church there. Each diocesan bishop is the principal teacher and governor of the Church in that locality. Worldwide, all the bishops, together with the Pope, are the official witnesses to the faith of the whole Church and responsible for her life throughout the world.

31. What is an ecumenical council?

It is an assembly of the whole Church under the leadership of the Pope. In modern times it has been almost entirely made up of the bishops of the Church.

32. What is infallibility?

It is a gift of the Holy Spirit by which the Church's faith is protected from error.

(2) Baptism

The Church is Jesus Christ become a way of life. What Christians believe about him, how they relate to him, how they think their lives should reflect his teaching—all this has been worked out in considerable detail over the centuries so that there is at hand a practical expression of the Christian faith in terms of human living. Like that faith, this way of life is never perfectly expressed but is caught up in some measure with particular historical and cultural peculiarities.

Despite these limitations, for the believing Christian the Church is the only place where he can live out his faith to the fullest. He needs to hear the Gospel again and again. He needs to be a part of the continuing work of Jesus in the world. And he needs the company of his fellow Christians as he grows in faith, takes his place in Jesus' mission, and celebrates what God has done for man.

To come to belief in Jesus is to come to the Church. To enter the life of Jesus, one enters into the life of the Church. Faith may come quietly from within, but the Christian response to it is quite public. The man who recognizes his Father in Jesus comes to the Church and asks for baptism.

1. How does a person enter the Church?

By a new birth. This time a person is born into the life of God. Simultaneously, he joins the community of Jesus' followers who share that life with him (John 3:1-4).

2. How does the new birth take place?

Through baptism and the Spirit (John 3:5-8).

3. What is baptism?

Baptism is a sacrament consisting of poured water and spoken words that together signify coming to life in God.

4. What is the significance of water?

It's a sign of life-giving and of cleansing. Life on this earth probably originated in its waters, and water is universally used for washing.

5. What is the significance of the words?

They signify that the life the person enters is that of God—Father, Son, and Holy Spirit.

6. What is the role of the Spirit?

The Holy Spirit unites us to Jesus so that we share with him the life of God he brought into the world.

7. What is the result of baptism?

A person is reconciled with God: his sins are

forgiven, he receives the life of God, and becomes part of God's people (John 3:16-17).

8. How is reconciliation possible?

In Jesus Christ God and man have been reconciled. Baptism unites the new Christian so closely to Jesus that he shares in his death and resurrection. Through this sacrament he dies to his old self and rises to new life (Rom. 6:1-11).

9. What is necessary for baptism?

Faith in Jesus Christ and the desire to follow him with his Church (Acts 8:35-39).

10. What is confirmation?

It is another sacrament that confirms or strengthens the life of the Spirit received at baptism.

11. How is it given?

The principal sign here is made by the bishop as he extends his hands over the confirmed and prays that the Holy Spirit come upon them.

12. Why are people confirmed?

To strengthen them in the mature and

responsible discharge of their mission to bear witness to Jesus Christ and serve their fellow men.

(3) The Sacrament of the Eucharist

Baptism begins the Christian life. It initiates man into the life of the Father, Son, and Holy Spirit. Their vital presence and love floodlights human living and rolls back its limitations. A sense of belonging to the Father of all creation, a realization of deeper purpose and importance in all that one does, a desire to stretch out for the fullest possession of the Father's gifts—these are some of the qualities that make the life of faith so liberating and attractive.

But baptism is only a start. There is a whole life to be lived after it. The Christian must continually come awake to that life and grow ever more alive with it. All man's faith-activities offer possibilities for this kind of revitalization—prayer, the sacraments, hearing the Word of God, Christ-like service of others, etc.

Some of these are more important than others. Of them all, the most important and indeed the central act of the Christian Church is the sacrament of the eucharist, or the Mass. In this great celebration of their common faith, Jesus' followers relive the experience of him and thank their Father for it. At Mass each Christian remembers who he is and what his Father has given him. At the same time, he receives again the same gift of Jesus Christ and enters more deeply into union with him in the Holy Spirit. Mass is the place where the Christian community both acts out its faith and is renewed and strengthened in all its members.

(a) THE EUCHARIST AS MEMORY

1. What is the Mass?

It is the Church's way of doing what Jesus did at the Last Supper (I Cor. 11:23-26).

2. Why does the Church do this?

In order to remember Jesus and to have a reunion with him.

3. What did Jesus do at the Last Supper?

He gave bread and wine to his apostles to eat and drink, telling them that it was his own body and blood. He then asked them to remember him always by doing this same thing among themselves (Luke 22:14-20).

4. How does the Church do this at Mass?

The Church recreates the Last Supper by bringing followers of Jesus together and recalling through readings and prayers what

God has done for his people. Then the priest
announces what Jesus said and did at the Last
Supper and himself offers bread (and, on some
occasions, wine) to the people to eat.

(b) THE EUCHARIST AS JESUS' ACTION

5. What was the effect of what Jesus did at the Last Supper?

His words and power made him really present
in the bread and wine that he gave his apostles
to eat so that they actually received Jesus in that
meal and were united with him (John 6:48-59).

6. What did this do to the apostles?

It made them one with Jesus and all that he did.
They shared his gift of himself to his Father
on the cross and in the Father's gift of life to
Jesus in the resurrection (I Cor. 10:14-21).

7. Does the Mass do more than remember Jesus?

Yes. Jesus himself is more than a memory.
Through his resurrection he is present and active
among us in his Spirit. The Mass is the place
where the Church not only remembers Jesus but
actually brings him and his saving death and
resurrection into the present so that his followers
may become part of it.

8. How can the Church do this?

Because Jesus is united to his Church in the Holy Spirit. When the Church celebrates the eucharist, Jesus is really there, and it is he who does once more what he did at the Last Supper.

(c) THE EUCHARIST AS JESUS' PRESENCE

9. How is Jesus present at Mass?

In several ways. He is present in his Word as the people listen to the Scripture readings. He is present in the priest and in the people through whom he acts to do again what he did at the Last Supper. And he is also present in a real way in the bread and wine that symbolize his body and blood.

10. How else does the Church express this presence of Jesus in the eucharist?

By preserving the consecrated bread and in the ceremony of benediction.

11. What is reservation of the blessed sacrament?

At the end of communion the remaining consecrated bread is placed in the tabernacle and reverently preserved. Thus, the blessed sacrament of the eucharist is always available both as a continuing sign of Jesus' real presence among his people and as spiritual food for the sick and dying.

12. What is benediction?

It is a brief ceremony wherein the blessed sacrament of the eucharist is exposed to the people for reverence and adoration. It concludes with the priest blessing the people with the consecrated bread.

(d) THE EUCHARIST AS RITUAL

13. What are the main parts of the Mass?

The liturgy of the Word and the liturgy of the meal.

14. What is liturgy?

It is the Church's communal act of giving praise to God and making men holy.

15. What is the liturgy of the Word?

It is the part of the Mass in which the people speak to their Father and listen to his Word. It consists of prayers, hymns, Scripture readings and a sermon. It lasts from the beginning of Mass until the end of the Creed.

16. What is the liturgy of the meal?

It is the part of the Mass that reenacts in words and deeds what took place at the Last Supper. In this service the Christian people enter into Jesus' gift of himself to the Father and receive in turn the Father's gift to them of Jesus. This liturgy begins with the offertory and ends with communion.

17. What happens at the offertory?

Bread and wine are prepared for the eucharistic meal.

18. What is the consecration of the Mass?

This is the part of Mass that announces what Jesus did at the Last Supper. It reminds us that he gave thanks to his Father and offered bread and wine to his apostles to eat and drink as his body and blood. This announcement is surrounded by prayers that express its meaning in various ways.

19. What is the communion of the Mass?

It is the meal of consecrated bread that

nourishes us with the life of God and unites us to
Jesus and to one another.

(e) THE MANY FACETS OF THE EUCHARIST

20. Why is the Mass so important?

Because it brings together all of the gifts the
Father has given us in Jesus Christ. It brings into
our lives the very presence of Jesus, his
sacrifice of himself on the cross, and the new
life of the Spirit opened to us in his resurrection.

21. How is the Mass a sacrifice?

It brings into the present Jesus' own offering of
himself to his Father on the cross. By doing this
in memory of him, we enter into that offering and
become a part of it.

22. How does the Mass bring us Jesus' resurrection?

Jesus' sacrifice established a common life of
friendship and love between the Father and his
children. Just as we share in Jesus' death at
Mass, so do we also share in the new life of the
Holy Spirit poured out on Jesus in his
resurrection.

23. What important human things are present at Mass?

All the basic human religious expressions: prayer, thanksgiving, worship, community, love.

24. How is the Mass a prayer?

It is a prayer to the Father in which his people give him thanks and praise for the wonderful future he has given us in his Son Jesus Christ. There are also times in the Mass in which we ask forgiveness for our sins and beg the Father's blessing upon ourselves and our fellow men.

25. How is the Mass thanksgiving?

By remembering what Jesus did at the Last Supper and doing it with him, the Church thanks the Father for opening his life to us.

26. How is the Mass worship?

By entering into the self-giving life and death of Jesus, the Church joins him in giving to the Father the only perfect worship the world has seen.

27. How are community and love alive at Mass?

In drawing us to union with Jesus, our Father draws us closer to each other. The Holy Spirit guides our responses with God's own love. As an assembly of Jesus' followers, the eucharist is both an expression of that unity and love that binds us to each other and to Jesus and an action through which the bonds are intensified.

V

MAN'S RESPONSE TO GOD

(1) Man the Believer

Faith brings a new quality to human life. To believe is to become aware, if not clearly and continuously, at least dimly and haltingly, that God is an active participant in one's activities and concerns. These take on new value and enduring importance. The believer also senses that this is the way man is meant to live and that all the wonderful potential for life he feels within will develop best in response to the creative summons of God.

Such a life with God is also an adventure in self-discovery and growth. It includes a new form of communication called prayer and a new depth of concern for others called charity. It is a life that has its share of setbacks and disappointments, but they are temporary, for the life of faith is nourished by the very life of God. It gives a person a handhold on the very source of life.

That is why the Christian places his give and take with God highest among his goals and aspirations and measures all else by it. It is also why in spite of difficulties and even apparent failure the Christian always has room for joy. His life is plugged into God.

1. What is faith?

Faith is what happens to man when he truly hears the Word of God. It is a free gift by which the Holy Spirit enables man to accept the Word completely and give himself and his life over to the Father (Rom. 10:8-17).

2. How is faith possible?

Only because God freely speaks his Word to man and at the same time opens man's mind and heart to his presence and love (John 6:44-47).

3. What is the effect of faith?

Something called justification. This means that faith brings man from a stage of alienation from God into communion with him and with his fellow men in God (Rom. 3:21-28).

4. What is grace?

Grace is what happens to man when the Holy Spirit comes to live in him. The Spirit brings God's quality of life to man and all that he does. So profound is the effect of this that thereafter a person is said to live in the "state of grace" (Eph. 2:4-10).

5. How does the Spirit come to man?

In many ways. He first comes from within in faith. Living as he does in the Church, he also comes through prayer and the Church's sacramental life. Finally, he also comes regularly through the people and situations and things that make up our lives (Rom. 8:28-30).

6. How does he bring men together?

By breathing God's own love into the human love and friendship and the yearning for them that brings men together and ties them to one another.

7. What is hope?

Hope is the realization that God cares and that we can count on him. It is the side of faith that enables us to see good in spite of evil and to expect life forever even in the face of death (Rom. 8:31-39).

8. What is the basis of hope?

Man can hope because in Jesus Christ God has committed himself to us forever and will never leave us if only we hang onto him.

9. What is charity?

Charity is the love of God and of our fellow men because they too belong to God (I John 4:12-21).

10. How is this kind of love possible?

Because God has given us his own love. The presence in us of the Holy Spirit means we are able to love with the love of God, even our enemies, if we will to do so (Rom. 5:5).

11. How important is charity?

It is everything. All of Christianity is love. God is love. His life is love. His kingdom is love. Man is created to love, grows through love, and finally finds himself by loving (I Cor. 13:1-7).

12. How can one tell the true Christian?

By the love he shows for his fellow man. Jesus said that this is how his followers can be identified (John 13:33-35).

13. What more does God ask of the believer?

Holiness or being like God. He wants us to be as much like him as possible. This means sharing more and more of our life with him so that he

can complete the good work he began in us
when he first spoke to us (Matt. 5:48).

14. From whom is holiness expected?

From the whole Church. Giving himself to all,
God makes it possible for everyone to give
himself completely to him and to his fellow man.
This doesn't mean that everyone gives himself in
the same way, for people are different, but it
does mean that all are called to holiness
according to the gifts and talents each
possesses.

15. What is a saint?

Saints are those whom the Church has declared
to be true models of holiness and worth
imitating.
(Of course, there are many other people about
whom the Church has said nothing and whose
holiness is known only to God and a very few
others. These are saints too, even though they
have not been declared so.)

16. What is necessary for holiness?

An openness to God and a willing response to
the guidance of his Holy Spirit (I Thess. 5:12-22).

17. What is prayer?

Prayer is communication with the Father, Son, and Holy Spirit. In prayer, man turns to God and listens for his Word. As God's Word takes hold in him, he learns to answer with words of his own.

18. What is the principal Christian prayer?

The eucharist. Here God's people gather both to hear his Word and to receive the Word made flesh and to express their thanks and praise.

19. How does a person pray?

One can pray with a group or alone; in words or in silence; kneeling, standing, sitting, or prone; in church or out; these are all incidental circumstances. The essence of prayer is conversation with God (Matt. 6:5-8).

20. What can we pray about?

We can pray about everything. God loves us enough so that whatever is important to us is important to him. We always have something for which to give him thanks and praise. Often there are things for which we are sorry. And he invites us to ask him for everything.

21. For whom should we pray?

For everyone. For ourselves, our families and friends; our enemies; the poor, sick and suffering; the dead and the dying; the whole Church; suffering nations; the list is endless. It is good to vary these subjects of prayer from day to day so as not to become mechanical about them.

22. How often should we pray?

Regularly. Daily, if possible, for when communication is weak or infrequent, people tend to forget the other person and drift away from him.

23. What form of prayer can be used?

Any form that is used by the Church or that the person praying finds helpful can be used. The best form we have is Jesus' own prayer, the "Our Father" (Matt. 6:9-15).

24. To whom should we pray?

All prayer is finally to God, and most of our prayers will be directed that way. However, sometimes we like to address the Blessed Mother or a saint and ask them to join especially in our prayer.

57

25. What role does sickness and suffering play in the life of the Christian?

Sickness and suffering offer the Christian the possibility of being a special witness to the sufferings of Jesus. By joining his own suffering to that of Jesus, what is a burden becomes a source of spiritual growth and liberation from self (II Cor. 12:7-10).

26. What is the sacrament of the anointing of the sick?

It is an act of the Church by which, through prayer and the anointing of the senses with blessed oil, a person who is seriously ill is strengthened in a special way by the Holy Spirit. This sacrament is also called "extreme unction" (Jas. 5:14-18).

27. What is the effect of the anointing of the sick?

The sick person's suffering is joined to the sufferings of Jesus, his sins are forgiven, and sometimes he is physically healed as well. If his sickness is final, then the sacrament strengthens him for death and prepares him for heaven.

(2) Christian Marriage

Faith not only introduces new activities and strengths

58

into the life of man but it also gives new depth to some familiar human institutions.

Marriage is one of these and this shouldn't surprise us. Anything expressive of love is already a reaching out to God, and we should expect God to use man's efforts at selflessness to draw him ever more deeply into his own life. And so he does.

Marriage is a lifelong partnership of love. It schools people in self-giving and sacrifice. It creates a climate of care for the raising of children. It educates the young to cooperation and concern for others. Of such materials is the kingdom of heaven constructed, and Jesus, knowing the best that is in man, has so vitalized human marriage that it is for the Christian a basic expression and realization of his faith.

1. What is Christian marriage?

A man and woman totally sharing life, love and Christian faith with one another and with God.

2. What is special about Christian marriage?

It is a sacrament. In this case, the human relationship of marriage is the sign through which God shows his love and communicates his life.

3. How is marriage a sacrament?

The Holy Spirit breathes God's own love into
the love between husband and wife so that each
becomes a grace for the other. As a result their
many acts of self-giving not only strengthen their
life together but also cause them to grow in the
life of God.

4. How does the sacrament of marriage show God's love for man?

By showing how close Jesus is to his people.
St. Paul tells us that marriage is a sign of the
relationship between Jesus and his Church. In
this best human example of love we see how
deeply Jesus is committed to his followers
(Eph. 5:21-33).

5. How is the sacrament of marriage given?

It is given first through the mutual promises
between husband and wife in the marriage
ceremony. Thereafter it continues to be given as
these promises are carried out in the years of
married life.

6. Who administers the sacrament?

The couple themselves. As they selflessly share
their life in God, the husband is the minister of

God's grace to the wife and the wife to the husband.

7. What is the function of the priest at a marriage?

He officiates at the ceremony as the Church's witness to this act of grace.

8. What is the goal of marriage?

The fulfillment and creation of human life. Through their mutual love the couple help each other and their children to become fully what God created each to be. At the same time, through the sexual expression of their love they become partners with God in the creation of new life.

9. What is a married couple's responsibility for new life?

Each couple must determine in the light of all the circumstances of their married life what is the unique creative partnership God invites them to share with him.

10. How does a Christian couple plan their family?

Through a conscientious assessment of what they should do to further the good of their whole family and of society. In this assessment they are helped by the teaching of the Church, their own knowledge of themselves and their family situation, and the example of other faithful Christians. As in all life decisions, here, too, people finally decide according to a well-informed Christian conscience.

11. How long does marriage last?

Marriage is for life. It lasts as long as both parties live (Mark 10:2-12).

12. Why is marriage permanent?

Because Jesus taught that married people should belong completely to each other just as he belongs completely to his Church.

(3) Man the Sinner

Faith changes human life but it doesn't take it away. Man, the believer, is still the same complex contradictory creature he has always been. He retains all of his freedom and his awful capacity for destruction. He continues to feel the pull of his own gravity, to be dazzled by his own gifts and powers, and to be tempted to exploit them regardless of consequences. In short, man, though reconciled to his loving Father in Jesus Christ, remains in some sense a sinner. His reconciliation is seldom total and never secure. While his commitment to Jesus may be very real and his life truly directed toward him, living this out is something else. The life of faith is marred by a thousand failures and compromises. Sometimes there is even a complete reversal of direction and the beginning of a way of life where the only commitment is to oneself.

No understanding of the Christian life can overlook the reality of man the sinner. At the same time no glimpse of man the sinner can ignore the luminous mercy of God's love that surrounds him. For the Christian to speak of sin is already to speak of forgiveness. He is all too aware of his own weaknesses and selfishness but he is even more aware of his Father's love. Sin is a reality for him but not a final one. For in Jesus Christ he knows that he has discovered his true self, and he also knows that, one day, sin will be finally taken away forever. Upon this conviction rests his Christian hope.

(a) Sin

1. What is sin?

Sin is saying "no" to God. Man sins when he refuses God's love and turns down his invitation to give of himself to God and his fellow men.

2. How is sin experienced?

Usually through personal acts of selfishness

that cause harm to others or to oneself. But often sin is experienced by **not** doing something—by refusing to move out of self toward others or to God. It can also be experienced through a passive acceptance of situations that are harmful or oppressive.

3. How is sin expressed?

Sin can be expressed in a person's thought, word, deed, or omission. Sometimes, too, when men's selfishness is widespread and persistent, sin becomes institutionalized and is expressed in the very structures of society so that its destructive power is multiplied many times over (Matt. 5:21-48).

4. Who is guilty of sin?

Since selfishness seems to be universal, all men presumably are guilty of some sin (Rom. 3:9-18).

5. How did sin begin?

Sin began when man first refused dependence upon God (Rom. 1:18-23).

6. When did this happen?

At the very beginning of man's existence. The Bible's account of Adam and Eve is the way in

which God's people reconstructed the beginning
of sin (Gen. 3).

7. **What was the effect of this first sin?**

Death and alienation from God. Thereafter men
are born into this world alienated from their
loving Father and subject to death. The Church
calls this situation "original sin" (Rom. 5:12-14).

8. **Who is subject to original sin?**

All men except Jesus. In God, the Son can
never be alienated from the Father. Also, by a
special grace Mary was born free of original sin.
This grace is called the "immaculate
conception."

9. **What is mortal sin?**

Mortal sin is a rejection of God so fundamental
that it destroys the life shared between God and
the sinner.

10. **What is venial sin?**

All lesser refusals by which man falls short of
what God asks of him.

11. What is the effect of mortal sin?

Separation from God and damage to oneself and others. Where the refusal is fundamental and remains unchanged, the separation is permanent. The Church calls this permanent estrangement from God "hell."

12. What is the effect of venial sin?

Damage to self and others.

13. Why is sin so damaging?

Man can only find his true self in a process of give and take with others. To do this he must come out of himself and give as well as receive. If he doesn't he undermines those relationships with others by which man lives and so ultimately destroys himself.

14. What is the main sign of sin in the world?

Death and particularly the death of Jesus Christ who came to give life. In this terrible event we see men literally rejecting God.

15. What are some other signs of sin?

War, poverty, hunger, racism, violence and other

persistent injustices are all signs of man's continuing sinful condition.

(b) Commandment, Law and Conscience

16. How does man learn of sin?

Through his experience of God. When man comes to know God, he also learns something about himself. God's light makes him aware of areas of darkness in himself, in others and in society.

17. Who taught man about sin?

In the Old Testament the Law of Moses was the principal teacher. In the New Testament the moral teaching of Jesus and his Church makes men aware of sin (Rom. 7:7-12).

18. What is the Law of Moses?

The Law is popularly summarized in the Ten Commandments. However, these are only a part of it, and the Jews consider the first five books of the Old Testament to be "the Law." They are so called because much of the foundation and life of God's people described there is in terms of law and obligation (Ex. 20:1-17).

19. What is the moral teaching of Jesus?

It is summed up in the two commandments he gave his Church: "You shall love the Lord your God with your whole heart, with your whole soul, and with your whole mind, and you shall love your neighbor as yourself." Many of Jesus' other statements and stories are examples of how these commandments work out in practice (Mark 12:29-31).

20. What is the moral teaching of the Church?

The Church continues teaching what Jesus taught and also studies the ever changing conditions of human life in the light of the Gospel so as to help men discover what God asks of them in every situation.

21. How does the Church express her teaching?

In different ways. The Church teaches by affirming specific ideals, by making judgments about the morality of common human actions, and by enacting laws covering some kinds of human behavior.

22. Are some acts sinful?

Not by themselves, for human acts cannot be separated from the person who does them. However, anything that is destructive to oneself or others is **wrong**; it may also be **sinful** if the person doing it knew it was wrong and intended it anyhow.

23. What kinds of acts are destructive?

Generally, (a) those which cause harm to a person, his property or his reputation—e.g., murder, theft, slander, etc.; (b) those which ignore the legitimate calls of others upon us— e.g., indifference to suffering, failure to worship God or pray, rejection of friendship, etc.; (c) those which betray a relationship with God or neighbor—e.g., disbelief, adultery, disobedience, etc.; (d) those which hinder one's own growth in love and responsibility—e.g., hatred, sexual activity apart from marriage, drunkenness, etc.

24. How can a person recognize sin?

Conscience enables a person to recognize when he acts sinfully. However, we can never know with certainty about others because we only see the outside of what people do.

25. What is conscience?

Conscience is an inner awareness of what God is asking a person to do in the present circumstances (I John 3:19-22).

69

26. How do I know whether my conscience is right?

I don't. However, over a period of time one can train his conscience through listening to the Word of God in the gospels and in the Church and by being attentive to the inspiration of the Holy Spirit within himself. Over a lifetime one's conscience so developed learns to recognize the call of God in every situation and aids a person to respond faithfully to him.

(c) Repentance and Forgiveness

27. What is the remedy for sin?

The remedy is Jesus Christ who came into the world to save his people from their sins. By participating in his death and resurrection, man triumphs over sin and death (Rom. 5:9-11).

28. How does man receive this remedy?

Through repentance and forgiveness.

29. What is repentance?

Repentance is a change of heart whereby the sinner turns back to God and accepts his loving forgiveness which God never refuses.

30. How can man repent?

Through the grace of God who, in spite of man's refusals, continues to speak to him.

31. How are repentance and forgiveness expressed in the Church?

Through the sacrament of penance.

32. What is the sacrament of penance?

It is an act of grace in which a person, having repented of his sin, confesses to a priest, receives absolution and does penance.

33. What is confession?

Confession is an act of faith in God's mercy in which a person acknowledges his sinfulness to God and to his people in the person of the priest.

34. What is absolution?

Absolution is the words of forgiveness spoken by the priest in confession. They are the sign of assurance of God's forgiveness.

35. What does it mean to "do penance"?

Doing penance is the performance of the acts of prayer or charity assigned by the priest in confession or voluntarily undertaken by the penitent. It Is a way of acting out repentance and strengthening the relationships with God and our fellow men damaged by sin.

36. What is purgatory?

It is the way in which these relationships are strengthened after death when a person has neglected penance in his life.

37. What is the purpose of the sacrament of penance?

To make visible and present God's mercy and forgiveness. In this sacrament the sinner can readily join himself to Jesus, dying to sin and selfishness and rising with him to new life with God.

38. What is the effect of the sacrament of penance?

Reconciliation with God and his people.

(4) Christian Man: Servant and Witness

Translating the Christian faith into a style of life is not

*easy. Beautiful truths and impelling ideals it offers
in abundance, but at times these are so lofty as to
overwhelm us. Yet each person who really believes in
Jesus Christ knows that he must reshape his life to
the Gospel. How to go about this? How does one
organize the activities and direction of a human life
in Gospel terms? What kind of occupation is "being
Christian"? What style of life should a man follow?*

*Over the centuries God's people have found different
ways of answering these questions. A long-time
favorite has been to follow the example of the monk
in the desert. The earnest Christian tried to arrange
his life to match that of the monk insofar as this was
possible. He withdrew from involvement in worldly
affairs beyond what was absolutely necessary. He
prayed the way they prayed in the monasteries. He
fasted regularly and denied himself luxuries the way
the monks did. He looked upon his life as a necessary
period of preparation for his life with God in heaven
and devoted a large share of his energy to the
preparation. In so doing his Christian faith became
alive and real.*

*Today, however, withdrawal from the world is not
really possible. Modern communications and
technology have thrust us all together in such a way
that the world is always a very big part of our lives.
The monastic model of Christian living does not fit
this situation very well, so the Church has dug into
her long experience and come up with a different
model for modern man: the model of the servant-
witness. Today we are challenged to design our lives
so that they bear witness to God by serving the
needs of man.*

73

This model calls for a life lived very much in the world and for the sake of the world. It calls for man to serve God by serving his fellow man. It calls upon Christians to live for others as Jesus lived and died for all. Such a life calls for a lot, but it promises to make the faith of today's Christian alive and real.

1. Why must Christians be servants?

Because Jesus was. His purpose in coming among men was to serve (Matt. 20:25-28).

2. Who is asked to be a servant?

Jesus calls his whole Church and each of his disciples to follow his own example of service (John 13:12-17).

3. What does it mean to be a servant?

The Christian servant, like his Master, is dedicated to others—concerned for their needs and ready to give of himself freely in response to them.

4. What forms of service are open to the Christian today?

The Christian can serve his fellow man directly by personally ministering to his spiritual, physical, and social needs, or he can serve him indirectly by working to better the society in which he lives.

5. **What are some examples of personal ministry?**

A Christian can effectively serve his fellow man through the ministries of medicine, nursing, teaching, preaching, social work, counseling and many other activities that heal in one way or another. These ministries can be full-time and professional or they can be limited and non-professional, according to the skills of the person who serves.

6. **What are some examples of social ministry?**

Service to man in society can be carried out in the fields of government, economics, law, business, education, environmental control, public health, and many other special services that enrich the fabric of the society in which men live.

7. **Must every Christian engage in these ministries?**

Every Christian must be a servant, but it is not possible for all to serve professionally. Each ministers according to the gifts and talents he has received (I Cor. 12:4-11).

8. How does the Church act as a servant?

The Christian community serves the larger
human community by sharing with it the riches
of its faith and cooperating in works that
express the common concern of all men for the
welfare of the human family.

9. What is Christian witness?

Christian witness is giving testimony to the
loving presence of God in the world.

10. How do Christians give this witness?

By their very existence as a community of faith
and brotherly love, by their preaching of the
Gospel, and, most important, by their service
to others.

11. What is the connection between service and witness?

A life of service to others is the best revelation
of the loving presence of God in our world.
Serving our needs is the way God acts toward
men.

12. Why is this kind of witness so important today?

Because the modern world makes men ever

76

more dependent upon one another, and without the kind of love Jesus brought, this universal coming together could easily crush man and destroy him.

13. What is required of the servant-witness?

A universally open attitude that has room for all peoples and a desire to relate selflessly to them.

14. How is this brought about?

By practicing dialogue within and without the Church, and laboring with all men to build up human society.

15. What is the purpose of this dialogue?

Friendship with all men and perhaps eventually a brotherly love that is lived not only within the Christian community but one that is woven into the life of the entire human family. In this way the servant-witness people of God truly become a sign and instrument of intimate union with God and of the unity of all mankind.

VI

POSTSCRIPT

The Real Truth about God

Jesus also said, "A man had two sons. The younger said to his father, 'Father, let me have the share of the estate that would come to me.' So the father divided the property between them. A few days later, the younger son got together everything he had and left for a distant country where he squandered his money on a life of debauchery.

"When he had spent it all, that country experienced a severe famine, and now he began to feel the pinch, so he hired himself out to one of the local inhabitants who put him on his farm to feed the pigs. And he would willingly have filled his belly with the husks the pigs were eating but no one offered him anything. Then he came to his senses and said, 'How many of my father's paid servants have more food than they want, and here am I dying of hunger! I will leave this place and go to my father and say: Father, I have sinned against heaven and against you; I no longer deserve to be called your son; treat me as one of your paid servants.' So he left the place and went back to his father.

"While he was still a long way off, his father saw him and was moved with pity. He ran to the boy, clasped him in his arms and kissed him tenderly. Then his son said, 'Father, I have sinned against heaven and against you. I no longer deserve to be called your son.' But the father said to his servants, 'Quick! Bring out the best robe and put it on him; put a ring on his finger and sandals on his feet. Bring the calf we have been fattening, and kill it; we are going to have a feast, a celebration, because this son of mine was dead and has come back to life; he was lost and is found.' And they began to celebrate.

"Now the elder son was out in the fields, and on his way back, as he drew near the house, he could hear music and dancing. Calling one of the servants, he asked what it was all about. 'Your brother has come,' replied the servant, 'and your father has killed the calf we have fattened because he has got him back safe and sound.' He was angry then and refused to go in, and his father came out to plead with him; but he answered his father, 'Look, all these years I have slaved for you and never once disobeyed your orders, yet you never offered me so much as a kid to celebrate with my friends. But, for this son of yours, when he comes back after swallowing up your property—he and his women—you kill the calf we had been fattening.'

"The father said, 'My son, you are with me always and all I have is yours. But it was only right we should celebrate and rejoice, because your brother here was dead and has come to life; he was lost and is found' " (Luke 15:11-32).

1. Who are the people in Jesus' story?

The father is God, the lost son is man the believer, the elder son is man the unbeliever.

2. What does the story say about the father?

The father is a giver—he supports his sons and gives the younger half the estate when he asks for it. He is also a forgiver—when the lost son returns he receives him with open arms, asks no questions, makes no judgments, but simply embraces the son he loves.

3. What do we discover about the lost son?

He is weak and selfish and wants to go his own way. When he finds that he can't make it on his own, he comes back to his father.

4. What does the lost son have to offer his father?

Nothing. He doesn't even apologize until **after** his father embraces him.

5. What does the father offer?

Everything. He goes out to meet his son and not only receives him back into the family but holds a feast in his honor.

6. What do we see in the elder brother?

He can't stand so much generosity. His father is giving too much. He asks questions, makes

judgments, and resents his father's
unconditional love.

7. What is the lesson of the story?

The point of Jesus' little story is that we humans
are weak and selfish and often insist upon
going our own way. All that we take with us we
have received from our Father. Left to ourselves,
we end up with nothing. Yet in spite of this—
and here is the crucial truth of the Christian
faith—God loves us more than we can quite
believe and almost more than we can stand.

PROFESSION OF FAITH

I, _____, enlightened by divine grace, profess the Christian faith as it is taught and practiced in the Catholic Church.

The Apostles' Creed

I believe in God, the Father Almighty, creator of heaven and earth; and in Jesus Christ, his only Son, our Lord, who was conceived by the Holy Spirit, born of the Virgin Mary, suffered under Pontius Pilate, was crucified, died, and was buried. He descended into hell; the third day he rose again from the dead; he ascended into heaven, sits at the right hand of God, the Father Almighty; from thence he shall come to judge the living and the dead. I believe in the Holy Spirit, the holy Catholic Church, the communion of saints, the forgiveness of sins, the resurrection of the body, and life everlasting.   Amen.

I believe that this Church is the Church in which the fullness of God's revelation through his Son, Jesus Christ, abides. I believe that her college of bishops, with the Pope, the bishop of Rome, presiding at its center, continues to exercise in the world the authority for teaching and moral guidance given by Jesus Christ to his apostles for the salvation of men.

I further believe in seven sacraments, signs of worship through which the grace of the death, resurrection and ascension of Jesus Christ is communicated. They are: baptism, confirmation, holy eucharist, penance, anointing of the sick, holy orders, and matrimony.

I promise, through prayer, participation in Church life and worship, and continued efforts to understand the tenets of my faith, to form my conscience in such a way as to live according to the doctrines and practices which the Roman Catholic Church prescribes for the individual and common good of her faithful.

The Lord's Prayer

Our Father, who art in heaven, hallowed be thy name; thy kingdom come; thy will be done on earth as it is in heaven. Give us this day our daily bread; and forgive us our trespasses as we forgive those who trespass against us; and lead us not into temptation, but deliver us from evil. Amen.

The Hail Mary

Hail Mary, full of grace! The Lord is with thee; blessed art thou amongst women, and blessed is the fruit of thy womb, Jesus. Holy Mary, mother of God, pray for us sinners now and at the hour of our death. Amen.